WEBLINES

John Agard was born in Guyana and came to Britain in 1977. He has published two collections with Serpent's Tail, *Mangoes and Bullets* and *Lovelines for a Goat-Born Lady*, and two with Bloodaxe, *From the Devil's Pulpit* (1997) and *Weblines* (2000). He is a popular children's writer whose titles include *Get Back Pimple* (Viking), *Laughter is an Egg* (Puffin), *Grandfather's Old Bruk-a-down Car* (Red Fox), *I Din Do Nothing* (Red Fox), and *We Animals Would Like a Word with You* (Bodley Head), which was shortlisted for the Kurt Maschler Award and won a Smarties Award. A new collection of his children's poems, *Points of View with Professor Peekaboo*, is due from Bodley Head in 2000. His recent anthology *Hello New*, published by Orchard Books, has been chosen by the Poetry Society as its Children's Poetry Bookshelf Best Anthology for the summer term of 2000.

He won the Casa de las Américas Prize in 1982 for *Man to Pan*, and in 1997 was one of the five poets given the Paul Hamlyn Award for Poetry.

As a touring speaker with the Commonwealth Institute, he visited nearly 2000 schools promoting Caribbean culture and poetry, and has performed on television and around the world. In 1989 he was awarded an Arts Council Bursary and in 1993 became the first Writer in Residence at London's South Bank Centre, who published *A Stone's Throw from Embankment*, a collection written during that residency. In 1998 he was writer-in-residence for the BBC with the Windrush Project.

He has also written plays. He lives with the poet Grace Nichols and family in Sussex.

JOHN AGARD

WEBLINES

BLOODAXE BOOKS

ISBN: 1 85224 480 1

First published 2000 by
Bloodaxe Books Ltd,
P.O. Box 1SN,
Newcastle upon Tyne NE99 1SN.

Bloodaxe Books Ltd acknowledges
the financial assistance of Northern Arts.

Cover printing by J. Thomson Colour Printers Ltd, Glasgow.

Printed in Great Britain by
Cromwell Press Ltd, Trowbridge, Wiltshire.

for Grace

Acknowledgements

I'm particularly indebted to folklorist Harold Courlander's *A Treasury of African Folklore* and *The Hat-Shaking Dance and Other Ashanti Tales from Ghana*; Capt R.S. Rattray's collection and translation of Akan-Ashanti folktales; Robert D. Pelton's *The Trickster in West Africa: A Study of Mythic Irony and Sacred Delight*; Amy Cruse's *The Book of Myths for the Sky-god* corn-cob story; *Jump and Say! (A Collection of Black Storytelling)* by Linda and Clay Goss for the Twi praise song and Ashanti proverb; and Richard Inwards' *Weather Lore* for spider weather sayings.

Thanks to Andrew Salkey for his cannily spun *Anancy's Score* and *Anancy, Traveller*, published by Bogle-L'Ouverture Publications.

Thanks to Walter Jekyll for preserving Anancy's antics in *Jamaican Song and Story*; Louise Bennett for vocalising the Anancy thread Miss Lou style; James Berry for adding his spin to the Britain-based web; Jan Carew for being part of the Anancy galaxy; Stewart Brown for his transatlantic support.

Thanks to Kamau Brathwaite and Wilson Harris for first making me aware of the limbo dance/slaveship connection. Wilson, through one of his talks, conjuring up the image of limbo dancer as 'dismembered god'; and Kamau, through his well-known poem 'Caliban' ('limbo/ limbo like me/ stick is the whip/ and the dark deck is slavery').

Thanks to All-ah-We team Ken Corsbie, Marc Matthews and Henry Mootoo for a crucial grounding in space/stage webcraft.

Thanks to Spree Simon, Ellie Manette, Neville Jules, Bertie Marshall and all the pioneers of the birth of steel-pan; to Aubrey Bryan, panmaker, tuner and player for pan-word collaborations; to Cy Grant, for expounding the pan-mystico dynamics of the sound.

Thanks to Casa de las Américas, Havana, for the award and first publication of *Man to Pan*, and to Greenheart for *Limbo Dancer in Dark Glasses*.

Thanks to *Poetry Review* where 'Anancy's Thoughts on Colours' first appeared; and to Serpent's Tail for *Mangoes & Bullets*, where 'Anancy's Thoughts on Love' appears.

Thanks to Paul Taylor for the roguish snap; and to Satoshi Kitamura for the anansically apt drawings and cover.

Thanks to the Akan-Ashanti people for Ananse, spider-spirit, trickster-transfigurer.

Contents

from MAN TO PAN (1982)

164 When you talking pan
165 I ain't know head or tail
166 Lick pan
167 Beat it out man
170 was like a return to me
175 Scatter a handful of pan

COME DOWN NANSI

Longtime Back in the Beginning

Who gave word? Who gave word? Who gave word?
Who gave word to hearing?
For Hearing to have told Anansi
For Anansi to have told the Creator
For Creator to have made the Things?

TWI PRAISE SONG FOR SPIDER

who speaks
with a lisp of eloquence

who struts
with a limp of elegance

who blesses
with the cure of a curse

whose thin waist
contains a universe?

To Baby Nansi's Head

They say matter
cannot be created
or destroyed

they never said matter
cannot be constellated
for the sheer joy
of it

so out of the black hole
        of her navel
spider grandmother ma

        spun
   a galaxy

and from the tree
        of night

        the stars
   hung
out their glittering thread

which she bequeathed to baby Nansi's head

The Coin of Birth

Spinning mama squatted her hairy horizon
on a bed of atoms

and out of the gushing purse of her wombspace
I came screaming with the coin of birth

and midwife moon threw back her head
in recognition of the long-awaited one

spider's word incarnate on whose tongue
stories shall be twinkling currency

the one with the never-ending navel string
tying continents in umbilical knots

and as if to mark the marvel of my birth
I Nansi closed one mint-eye for mischief sake

my eight legs tapping epics from the cosmic floor

Flesh to Fancy

1

Nansi
Anansi
Ananse
Anancy
Nancy

however spell me
merely invoke me

and from my web-bed
I will rise

the eightlegged one
will take on twolegged guise

will answer to the name
of uncle or aunty

and give flesh to fancy

2

So
I spread open
my womanpart furrow
and wait for yam water
to make a harvest of my hip

Aunty Nansi say earthbelly magic
make manpart disappear

So
I stroke
my manpart digging stick
and resort to old incantation trick
singing praise to seed-sowing

Uncle Nansi say yam water music
keep womanpart growing

3

Cunning spread its dazzle rays
to trap cloud
in web of light

Trickery trickled from the underbelly

of a leaf

Wisdom winked from shift of green
mercury-eyed grass

And I Nansi preened
my spider costume
in morning's mirror.

Rain falling
Sun shining
Perfect day for shapeshifting

Anancy's Thoughts on Colours

(for Andrew Salkey)

Long-time back in the beginning beginning
when sky-god Nyame was handing out colour,
sky-god Nyame take one look at me Anancy
and say pick whichever colour you fancy.

I cast me eye high
I cast me eye low
I work up me brain to studify
dis colour issue,
spare it a thought or two.

Red stare at me from deep gash of skin
Yellow try to tempt me with sunflower grin
Green wink at me with brazen leaf-eye
White beckon me with subtle shift of cloud.
And all dis time blue so damn calm and proud
as if one shimmer and Anancy done blue.

I work up me brain good-good.
I turn to sky-god Nyame.
I say sky-god Nyame, I done ponder
dis thing you call colour issue.
Thank you but no thank you.

Let Snake, Tiger, Parrot and dem
hustle up for colour hand-out.
I will stay original dark
as it was in the beginning beginning,
spinning web of bright imagining,
cherishing the gift of cunning.

How Anansi Got Last Yam

Only one yam remaining
and Anansi must have it

No toss of coin
No roll of dice
No cast of lot
will decide it

Only one yam remaining
and Anansi will not divide it

‘Let the most deserving have it’
is the unanimous cry.

Then Anansi tell his classic lie
the yam so fattening his eye

‘I am the most deserving’ he says,
‘Can you not see I have my period?’

How Ananse's Waist Suffered a Double-Dine Dilemma

My waist wasn't always this thin.
Let me take you back to the beginning

when plump waist pillowed Spider's side.
Oh yes, I was quite a different size.

It all happened, if I'm honest,
because of my little food weakness

for all roads lead to the pot,
and I always say first come gets it hot.

So when news cordially reached me
of plans for big knees-up feed-up spree

in north town and south town, yes, all two,
I cogitated what to do,

for even with these eight legs of mine
I can't be in two places same time.

If I go north town feast, my mouth
will miss out on south town feed-out.

If I go south town wine-and-dine,
north town partake will pass me by.

So I devised a strategema
to deal with this double-dine dilemma.

Tying two long ropes round my waist
I said to my first son, make haste

take the end of this rope, go north town.
When feasting start, pull hard, I will come.

Then I summoned my second son
and gave him similar instructions:

Take the end of this rope, go south town.
When feasting start, pull hard, I will come.

With my two ropes and two sons
covering the feasts from both directions

The plan was to stay still and wait
for signal to sweet-mouth celebrate

How was I to know that both north and south
would simultaneously start sharing out?

Well, to cut a long story short,
those obedient boys pulled hard from south and north

you'd swear it was tug-o-war tussle
while I paid the price with my middle

which I'm pleased to say
lives on in legend and riddle.

How Worksong Call-and-Response Came To Be

Over riverside log
woman beating cloth
hand up and down
in sunwash rhythm

under selfsame log
Nansi makes no sound
thinking what to do
with his erection

when out of the blue
he spots a hole
cleaving straight through
the very living log

as if skygod Nyame
with divine tact
had left an opening
for genital pact

and low and behold
through this doorway
Nansi slips man-rudeness
into woman-rudeness

and the air is ripe
with the wine of her hips
and to the beat of cloth
first worksong bursts from lips:

beatee-cloth
slowly-so
spider down below
aye-o gimme mo

beatee-cloth
wetty-so
spider down below
aye-o gimme mo

beatee-cloth
sweety-so
spider down below
aye-o gimme mo

To this day some folklorists argue
that worksong call-and-response is due
to humdrum cloth-beating repetition.

But Aunty Nansi and Uncle Nansi positioned
on a certain log would laugh ee-ee till they weep.
Before they turn over in antiphonal sleep.

How Anansi Won Who-Is-Oldest Contest

So Guinea Fowl
You say you born in time of first great fire
when the red beast devoured grass and earth.
And I don't doubt that your two feet got burnt
from stamping out the flames that left many dead.
To this day I see your so-so legs still red.
Guinea Fowl, you're no spring chicken I agree,
for there you stand on heroic proof Eee-eee-eee.
But wait till you hear Nansi testimony.

So Parrot
You say you born in a world without weapons
and even tools were nowhere near fashioned.
No spear or knife to strike an enemy.
No axe to ground a standing tree.
Nothing to keep a blacksmith busy.
Not till your beak became the first hammer
to beat iron into shape. That was clever.
I'm not surprised your beak got bent Eee-eee-eee.
Even your speech seems a little misshapen.
The price paid for playing blacksmith in feathers.
But as for age, leave that to your spider elders.

So Elephant
You say you witnessed sky-god Nyame's first word
that breathed into clay a fourfooted shape
and each and every animal found a name.
Now, Elephant, that's a marvellous claim.
And that nose of yours, a prodigious feature,
sky-god pronounced before all other creatures.
Well, that explains the nose-material shortage
and why spider folk like me Eee-eee-eee
were shortchanged in breathing appendage.
And who'd dare doubt Elephant's memory?
But in age, big boy, you're still a baby.

Let Nansi
update you three on point of precedence.

My small nose breathed in all eternity.
My mouth spin with thread a song of iron.
My legs double-embrace the four directions.
I was there when night and day were untwinned
and world was barely beginning to begin
and no earth made yet to stand on.
In such a groundless timeless time was Nansi born
that when my grandmother was pronounced dead
I had no spot to bury her in.
Yes, if it's proof of age you want Eee-eee-eee
Come close. Grandma grave still here inside me head.

How Wisdom and Commonsense Were Scattered

All wisdom must dance
only to my drum

All commonsense must play
only in my head

So wisdom
I gathered atom by atom

So commonsense
I gathered every thread.

Assembled the lot
into my largest gourdpot
which I planned to hide up the highest tree.

But with gourdpot on my belly –
even one full of wisdom and commonsense –
I couldn't for the life of me climb that tree.

From behind the bushes my youngest child called out:
'May I make a suggestion, Father?
I see you're having difficulty.
Put gourdpot on your back, then climbing is easy.'

Out of a child's mouth came the solution.
And just when I thought I had gathered every jot
of wisdom and commonsense into one gourdpot.

There and then I threw down
my gourdpot in downright vexation
and from the selfsame shattered pieces
all wisdom and commonsense
flew to every direction.

If you didn't catch any, foolish you.
If you catch any, thank me Nansi.

for your tiniest gossamer of gumption.

How Tiger Played Dead and How Anansi Played Along

One day Tiger hale and hearty,
stripes resplendent, body well fed.
Next day, Tiger take so poorly,
his wife say Tiger gone and dead.

Well, this news didn't ring too right,
at least not to my Anansi ears.
Tiger seemed free from mental cares
and showed no sign of failing might.

Wariness of mind may be my fault
but such tidings must be pinched with salt.
For while death comes on horseback, it's true,
Tiger can't dead just so out the blue.

Caution persuaded me to suspect
Tiger was staging his own death.
But I kept my thoughts to myself
and observed the turn of events.

Sure thing, Tiger and his madam
had jointly concocted up a plan
to have their hungry-belly way
with the small creatures of the land.

For when these came to mourn and pay
last farewell on that sad day,
Tiger planned to spring up from deceased
and play the true devouring beast.

The Tigers grinned and pre-set
their table for a funeral feast.
And Mrs Tiger lived up to her role,
putting on her best widow's mourn:

Tiger dead! My husband dead, Aye-o!
Here today, gone tomorrow
O life has dealt a cruel blow.
Welcome friends, share my sorrow.

Donkey, Dog, Goat, Pig, Parrot –
that whole inquisitive lot –
had gathered to commiserate.
Tiger meanwhile lying in state.

I sort of grieved on the sidelines
and decided to play my trump card.
I drew Tiger's grieving wife aside
and offered my condoled regards.

To all intents, you're a widow.
I take my hat off to your sorrow.
And no disrespect to your broken heart
but tell me truly, did Tiger fart?

So you come to mock, not pity me?
I am surprised at you, Anansi.
I assured her on the contrary,
for I had travelled widely

And no tiger really breathes its last
without a rite-of-passage fart.
Only after that final blast
can a dying tiger depart.

My words of course reached Tiger's ear
for I had spoken fortissimo,
and comforting the weeping widow,
I said Mrs Tiger have no fear

If your husband is yet to pass wind,
then he is still in the land of the living.
And Tiger unable to hold back
exploded from his bottom-crack.

A farting corpse, needless to say,
sent all creatures scurrying away.
Don't thank me, I said. Thank the wind.
And returned pronto to my ceiling.

The Coming of Debt

So a man comes to our village
running from debt.

We had seen people running
    from the jaws of leopard
    from the embrace of python
    from the pursuit of ghosts
    but from debt – Never.
For we had not known debt.

Now this man is carrying debt
on the slopes of his shoulder
in the furrow of his brow
and debt will not leave him be.

So I say to him I know how
you can get rid of your burden.
Simply repeat after me:
    What's mine is yours
    What's yours is mine
    Come rain Come shine
    Whoever drinks my palm wine
    Will take my debt.

Without hem or haw, he agrees
and Nansi happy as the birds and the bees.
See me flying back to my house
buzzing with his bowl of palm wine
but now carrying his debt
like a child on my hips
like a hump on my back.

With palm wine sweet on my Nansi lips
I stumble on a plan to shove off debt.
Right so, planting my fields,
I break into a sing-sing:

What's mine is yours
What's yours is mine
Come sun Come rain
Whoever eats my grain
Will take my debt.

Lo and behold, a bird plays bold.
Eats up my grain and off she flies
taking debt on the wind
taking debt to her nest.
Among her eggs debt now lies
as bird sings to her brood:
What's mine is yours
What's yours is mine
Two legs four legs
Whoever breaks my eggs
Will take my debt.

Soon a tree branch falls
and crack go the eggs.
Now it's your turn to carry debt
bird cries to the tree.
Because you have broken my eggs
you must find room for debt
among your leaves or bark
for debt is now tree's guest.

Not yet, not yet, tree objects.
True, I broke your eggs, but let's not forget
it's wind that stripped the branch from my side.

Now wind carries debt
in a gust-fall of pollen
and whispers debt's name far and wide
spreads debt from village to village
like a wayward message.
Yet I Nansi have no regrets.
For I relieved a stranger
running from debt
and this much we owe to debt –

fragile thread that tests the strongest friendship.

How Dance and Sores Spread Far and Wide

It was a morning made for song and dance
when I see this old woman in sunlit clearing
and her song to my ears was more beautiful than flybuzz
and her dance was mathematics defied beyond daring

teach me to sing and dance like you I beg her
for I was not backward in coming forward
and so she teach me the rudiments of her song and dance
till I was perfect copy of her sound and movement

Now my voice was all honey my waist all water
but what a itching and scratching possessed me
for though with song and dance she blessed me
now my skin was cursed with the gift of her sores

and after her skin was completely healed
she disappeared same way sudden as she had come
and still my Nansi feet a-turn and wheel
and still my Nansi voice a-rise and pitch

but let me say how I just couldn't stop itch
for everywhere over it's old woman's sores I feel
and as I sing and dance I scratch-so scratch-so
till finally I reach the next village

teach us to sing and dance like you Nansi
they begged me as they watched in wonder
so I teach them the way the old woman teach me
and soon their voice was all honey their waist all water

how they sang and danced and scratched all the more
as if their skin was a bed of running ants.
I thank you people for taking away my sores –
a small price to pay for song and dance.

How Anansi Helped Skygod Get One Hundred Slaves from Earth

Skygod wanted one hundred slaves from earth.
So I said to Skygod give me one corncob
and I will bring your desire, trust my word.

Skygod erupted into thunderous giggles.
Return empty-handed, you cheeky spinner,
and I'll make your waist even thinner.

Succeed and Anansi will be top-top spokesperson.
The one whose voice is heeded by the tribe
when spider reshuffles the divining bones.

So with corncob I descended on earth-slave quest.
At first village I received welcome for the night
and made sure corncob was well out of sight.

I tucked it high in roof-thatch for safe-keeping
but when the villagers were soundly sleeping
I slipped out and fed corncob to the fowls.

Next morning how I fussed, how I carried on:
O cursed be the ones who stole Skygod's corncob.
They will rue the day when Skygod rights this wrong.

I guess my histrionics did the trick
for they gave me a basket of corn so quick
you'd think Skygod had done sent vengeance.

At the crossroads I met a woman with an old goat
and she thought a basket of corn was fair barter.
There I struck an exchange without any palaver.

At second village they tied the goat in a pen,
saying Anansi, our much-travelled friend,
rest in the knowledge that your goat is secure.

So I pretended sleep while the others snored.
Then I crept outside, unroped the goat, shooed it free,
scattering a trail of goatdung to the chief's door.

Next morning I caused a stir, to put it mildly.
O misfortune on the ones who took that goat
for they have plundered Skygod's property.

Not wanting to tempt divine retribution
and fearing the goatdung trail might raise questions,
the chief said take ten of our sheep and be gone.

That was enough for me to stop my commotion.
So I continued my journey with ten sheep.
Along the way I could hear people wail and weep.

They were carrying a dead boy for burial
and their village I gathered was far away.
Here was the chance for me to have my say.

Before your journey's end, the body will rot.
Out of your pain, O people, why not make some gain?
Swop me the body for my ten sheep, it's all I've got.

They thought this exchange unusual, to say the least.
But in the end they went off ten sheep richer
and I, carrying a corpse, was heading east.

At nightfall I found a hut for the dead boy
and how the villagers sang and danced with joy
when they heard it was Skygod's sleeping son.

Into the hut I carried food which I myself devoured,
returning with empty bowls to please our hosts.
The boy has eaten, I said. He sleeps like a flower.

Indeed Skygod's son is such a deep sleeper
nothing could wake him. No drum, nightmare, cockcrow.
Only a good flogging makes him get up and go.

So at dawn I asked the chief's sons to wake their guest
but first reminded them to ready their whips.
And they spared no blow. They gave him their best.

O what have you done? I cried. The boy is dead.
And I ran outside bawling and beating my head.
O the chief 's sons have flogged Skygod's son to death.

This announcement put the chief in a panic.
How can we ever seek Skygod's forgiveness?
Advise us, Anansi, help us out of this mess.

So I wept. I pondered. I stalled for time.
I said I won't vouch for forgiveness of this crime
but one hundred slaves may partly recompense.

All this was long ago in mythic tense
when Skygod bowed to Spider's demands
and out of one corncob I wove an oracle

that houses with wings will walk on water
and carry off our sons and daughters
to the killing fields of distant lands.

Now shame sleeps like a guest under my roof
and because my kith and kin have lost their names
I must build a covenant of broken webs

for black and white hands have a deed to atone
as night and day are woven warp and woof.
I Anansi have spoken with the breath of bone.

When Water Was All the Talk in the Rafters of History

Even the Cloth Can Talk

PROVERB WOVEN ON KENTE CLOTH, ROYAL
FABRIC MADE BY THE ASHANTI WEAVERS

everspinning grandmother Ma opened
        wide as first laughter
and out crept the Word and the Word was moist
        and the Word ran
down mountainside and over dry rock
and mountainside wept and dry rock trickled
        as never before in the beginning
and on that miracle of a morning
        a new noun was given good homecoming

Water was all the talk

the Word
grew eight legs

and spiralled
in a womb
of water

darkness pulled
new growth
from every corner

and making
of her mouth
a shuttle

spider grandmother
spat out
her rope ladder

that joined
a star
to eye of clay

mesmerising all
with rise and fall
of water

that would know
no boundary

even then I knew water
would be a mixed blessing

by water dispossessed
by water renewed

nameless ones going under
a limbo of ocean

to reclaim lost limbs

The stranger's cloth billows on water.
A sadness swells in the wind.
Narrow strips of totemic colour
give way to an all-pervasive blue
and iron hold of darkness

No leap of antelope
through grassland warp
No creep of python
through length of loom
Gone the woven ancestral patterns
that keep heart anchored
to patchwork harmony

Now the stranger's cloth
that hides its soul
and speaks no word of homecoming

But did you think I'd desert you so easy
my diasporic spiderlings
my siblings of the web

No I stowed away in the ceiling
of your dreams whose waters
the big ships could not chart

And in your utmost imaginings
I began new weavings

spinning rainbow cloths from history's rubble

Small voices weep
for kinship webs
broken by iron chain

Feel the golden stool
shift from the seat
of your dreams

Heaved into new horizons
by the power
of a stranger's cloth

Bought on a block
without birth markings
or libation

Branded by
a baptism of ocean

Ocean caul
Ocean shroud
Ocean flag
Ocean robe

Show me Ocean
your hidden seams
where rocks keep vigil
and I'll unravel
memory's cloth.

Eight-limbed star
see-far avatar.

When the palm leaf chips
are cast to the ground

and the oracle slips
from Ananse's tongue

the spider prophet
will reveal the score

that unsettles thrones
and tests dominions

with destiny's thread.

water stand up
water lay down

and the old sugarcane riddle
takes on new meaning

what secrets do they whisper
from middle passage history

these green members
of my extended family

leaning their stiffness
on the wind's shoulders

a far bleeding cry
from the staff of elders

these knotted gods know no rest
till the blood sacrifice

and libation of sweat
stain their altars of sweetness

and the old sugarcane riddle
takes on new meaning

water lay down
won't stay down

for at burning time
embers of leaves

take to the sky
like an uprising of spiders

where whispers fill
the conch shell's throat

where the seaweed takes note
of the uncounted dead

where waves rattle their gourds
for the unmourned ones

someone must translate water's sub-text

and is so Ananse's thread of thought

                unwinds
across the ocean's warp

and makes a ceiling
of your inner head

from grandmother Ma
cosmic seamstress
I learn my spinning ways

and since old habits
die hard

out of scattered limbs
I will forge a loom
refuse to make an icon
of doom

and in the mouths of exile
I will spin proverbs
bridging two worlds

teach transplanted ones
the weaver's way with words

Hide talking drum
in skin of English words

Fetch rainwater vowels
in goblet of mouth

Pound yam of consonants
with pestle tongue

Prepare throat
as thatched roof
for sibilant breezes

Serve up language mix
Moonlight talk
with darkcover classics

Spinning thread from ear
to page

in sunweb of steel I squatted

and new melodies spiralled
from old drumbeats

in limbo I dismembered my godself

and from old brutalities
new beings emerged

in time's cosmic courtroom

where truth and lies
shake their loom

I weave between the lines

playing fool to catch wise

and in the rafters of history

I spin webs
to catch those footnote-flies
that buzz
with more than eyes
could read

Ceiling Thomas
I am nicknamed

So I put on my mask
and play the game

of the doubting outsider
the doubleminded spider

who puts a finger
in history's sides

for proof of blood
for remnant of song

The diasporic dice
like the ships
are loaded

but there's many a slip
between teeth and tongue

as there are hitches
in rope

and stitches
in cloth

not to mention
cracks
in cricket pitches

and messages
in talking drum

and webs
in ceiling

where oracles
are hoarded

and history's dice
unloaded

It's weaving time, my people

Gather your fragments
into fabrics

Gather your wanderings
into webs

Gather your threads
into tapestries

Gather your contradictions
into cloths of wholeness

Not on Holiday

When spiders' webs in air do fly
The spell will soon be very dry

TRADITIONAL WEATHER SAYING

The Embodiment

since spider feel at home
with thread and rope

I thought I'd try Eu-rope
(the name sounded promising)

so I headed for England
land of hope and unfinished glory
like Schubert's symphony

leaving Amsterdam to surinam spinners
and Paris to Martinique weavers

arrived at Heathrow not quite light
eight nothing-to-declare suitcases
balanced on eight metropolis-dreaming legs

soon got used to juggling eight cups of tea
like I was spider embodiment of Earl Grey

and nobody made any comment
till I metamorphosed into proper
tophat ascot gent

and bought a piece
of property in Kent

then the pauses
became pregnant

and I heard myself say

No I'm not on holiday
Spider is here to stay

Anancy's Thoughts on Clock

Short hour-leg.
Long minute-leg.
And that needle-thin
extra limb
twitching to nerve
of seconds.

Old three-legged timekeeper
Not like yours truly
eight-legged timeweaver
inviting all and sundry
into spider metaphysics.

Hours not measured
in hobbling ticks

but the web's still pendulum.

Dethatched

CHARMING LITTLE PERIOD
BEDWORDIAN COTTAGE
SEAMINGLY THATCHED
END-OF-TERRACE VIEW
OF TONGUE CENTRE
COMPLETE WITH SECRET
KNITTED KITCHEN
HIDE-DYLLIC FOR FIRST-TIME
SUBURBAN WEAVERS

Anancy's Thoughts on Hospitality

Let heart
be a hut
thatched with love

open to visitors
from below
and above

and when the stranger
calls to your door

even if there's no
room on your heart-floor
to spread
a sleeping mat

remember to say
(just in case)
say to the thin-waist
traveller who's leaving

Come back, friend,
you're welcome
to a corner
of my ceiling

and even
the fly
in my pot.

Board Games

Let grandmasters
grapple grey matter
with mind-challenging Chess.

Let capture mongers
test ambush manoeuvres
on battleground Draughts.

Let homeseekers
place faith in dice throw
for destination Ludo.

Let Mammon schemers
stock up paper money
for multi-storey Monopoly.

Let fortune dreamers
pin future plans
on lucky-hand Cards.

Let word dabblers
deal with Babel pieces
of word-smart Scrabble.

I'll have indoor fun
with Spiders and Ladders
weaving web to sky rung by rung.

How Nansi Got Lead Part in *Swan Lake*

Face-masked, nerves unwracked, stomach butterfly-free,
at audition time I presented my eightlegged mime
and white leotards swanleapt in spotlight

Soft as fufu I glided in the tutu that covered my cucu,
doing a pas-de-deux me one twice times over, true-true,
and pirou-eighted to make old spider grandmother proud.

They all agreed I was born for upstage swan part.

On first night I received standing ovation of flowers
followed by coronation of rave reviews.
To be honest, it was just a regular ruse.

But papers hailed my artistry as spellbinding.
First time ballet buffs had ever witnessed
ballerina swan transformed to spider gracefully unwinding.

Musicologist Anancy

This business of musical notation
can cause much aggravation

which may or may not pertain
to freeing up octaves from their chains.

Speaking as one with direct line to sky-deity
I personally have always moved freely
between basso profundo and falsetto

and consider ceiling, as you know,
to be the highest form of C.

So while others cut their dress
to suit their cloth, according to me Nancy,

I cut my notes to suit my pitch –
if you get my drift –
and leave the rest to history.

My Brollie

My grey suit matching English skies
I took a spiral stride
down the April pavements.

I had made a truce with rain
and almost felt Anglo-saxon.
My at-homeness was heaven-sent.

A bobby doffed his helmet
in my foot-weaving direction
and the pigeons kept their distance.

All the signs told me to dance
or at least open my brollie
like some forgotten icon

So whether clouds play foul or fair
I wave my brollie's royal web
and embrace the anonymous air.

Thirteen Ways of Looking at the Old Tie

A striped reminder
of the embers of empire.

*

A nostalgic neck-binder
for a post-colonial evening.

*

An emblem that divides
insiders from outsiders.

*

A prop for suicide
by way of strangulation.

*

An icon of Eton
worn even with the heat on.

*

A signifying signpost
to the nearest pubic station.

*

A crested spearhead
into male bonding.

*

A formal demarcator
of respect for the dead.

*

A diagonal entry
into the Royal Artillery.

*

A cross-sexual accessory
of gender-bending politics.

*

A Freudian substitute
for the umbilical cord.

*

A subliminal throwback
to the Neanderthal club.

*

In Nansi's motley wardrobe
the tie, on the other hand,

could be quite simply
a polka dot silk paddle

to row the sea of circumstance.

When Anansi Goes Walkies with Eight Dogs

Walkies with eight dogs on eight leash
is a skill I Nansi can teach
any canine-cuddling petlover of the sceptred isle

for it takes a certain guile, not to mention style,
to be the hub of a yelp-wagging mandala
and the centre of Hyde Park attention.

But see me in lilywhites catching dregs of summerlights
each leash stretched to barking point
children trailing me like Pied Piper

So I turn best friend to mongrel and pedigree yelper
and old smileridden folk offering free advice
on flea-control and bone-chewing issues,
for immigration matters are a world left behind.

Man, feeding eight dogs is expensive, to say the least,
but they make a wonderful conversation piece.
And when I throw my stick skyhigh with 'Fetch ya'
Hyde Park resounds with chorus of hallelu-jahs.

All Seasons Nansi

1

Call me a sucker
for daffodils
but I too flutter
when they tease the ear of March
with yellow tidings.
They fill me with blood-rush
till I am flush with Spring.
I go weak at the knees
and Wordsworthian at the mouth
when I see these happy hosts
dancing in a breeze.
I know that soon the sun will blossom
in the cheeks of England.

This is time
for Nansi to smile extra cute
and greet every face as passing flower
though not every flower bears fruit.

2

Summer brings its own buzz
and fizz of flesh flaunting by
and looking does more than feed the eye.
Under a marmalade sun
bodies spread themselves
to be toasted browner than brown.
Hayfever sufferers beware
the pollen in the air
but tan-seekers lay bare
layer by layer by layer.

This is time
for Nansi to sit in the shade
and ponder: does the leopard lose its spots?
Does the guinea hen lose its freckles?

3

November pavements
carpet-plush with fallen leaves
and treacherous wet.
Better mind your step,
all you who walk on two legs,
when autumn sheds its bounty.
Berries aplenty crushed underfoot
say severe winter is afoot.
Or as the old saying goes:
Spiders' webs afloat at autumn sunset
bring a night of frost, you bet.

This is time
for Nansi to say don't blame me
I'm only the bearer
of weather's prophecy.

4

Come winter, wherever you are,
send us your confetti
snowflakes that make brides of trees
and pretties up a city's scars.
Make ground fresh with snowflake crunch,
each one a tiny ice-flower
each one unique in a shower of millions.
Hello snowflake, ghostly hexagon
that speaks of shape-shifting water,
is it true that a fruitful spring
follows a rainy winter?

This is time
for Nansi to give thanks for cardigans
and to keep a little silknumber
tucked away in abdominal glands.

How Aunty Nancy Converts the Intruder

Look pon dis bwoy in balaclava mask.
Him cyant tell him face from him arse

but living up to the role of burglar
rummaging Aunty Nancy suburban space.

Now hear how she confront the intruder.
'Seek and you shall find the computer

Knock and my CDs shall show their silver
Ask and all my gold shall be yours

for currency is not the minting of money
but the coining of a shining phrase

so take all your youthful hands can gather
and I pray your mother forgive your ways

when she hear bout dis in tomorrow's tabloid.
Don't stand there speechless in a void.

Make haste, son, and do your business.
All you have is a spider for witness.

But remember even cloth could talk
And one day fine thread will arrest your steps.'

And so the youth run off with a curse.
His road back home his own Damascus.

The Nansification of NF

Strolling past sweet Thames softly-softly song
into an autumn evening's golden aura
Nansi spy through Nansi eye-corner

these two letters sprayed on a subway wall –
N and F coupled in bloody scrawl
a far cry from November's flourish.

While neon lights spelt out box-office charms,
there across a city's concrete heart
two letters formed a vile coat-of-arms.

Tiger in speech promotes the rule of stripes
– i.e. no fur, no fins, no feathers –
yet Tiger ain't the graffiti type.

No, this was the handiwork of human hands.
Hurried. Desperate. Nowhere half as neat
as a spider's dancing calligraphic feet.

How Nansi, who partial to fish and chips
and a firm believer in cricket,
go handle such mindless hieroglyphics?

And as in the beginning word was made flesh,
out of an NF void –
Nansi forward into Nansi future.

Aunty Nancy's Sound Check

(for Kwame Dawes for amplifying the aesthetics)

Music doctor sound
Aunty Nancy system
Music doctor nod
'Sound sound system.

Everything praise God
in good working order
despite so many crossings
of border after border.

Heartbeat clear as stereo
Pulserate regular treble
Cholesterol turned well low
Brain cells ringing decibels

Eyes and ears fully tuned
Belly ready for volume
Blood in line with bass line
Reflexes doing off-beat fine

Limbs syncopated
Organs orchestrated
Breathing in key with drum-shift
Every lisp reverbed remixed.

What's your secret, Aunty Nancy?'
Spider lady says with a grin
'I try to exercise my mind
on the dance floor of the ceiling.'

Anancy's Thoughts on Love

Love got teeth
as old people say
dont know if you walking
on you hand or you feet
but it dont really matter
cause you bound to meet
sooner or later

love is watching hint
big and bold
but refusing to catch it

love is trapping thoughts
in side-eye gaze
long before thoughts see light-of-day

love is sweet mystery
like sleight-of-rain

But love is sweet misery
like taste-of-pain

love is going down winding labyrinth
at loss for words
and loss of head
but Anancy thank God
always have piece of thread
for way back out

or to put it another way
Anancy in love
always save back piece of heart
for peace of mind

How Nansi Reigned Over a Royal Bath

Behold a spider
in the Queen's bathtub.
But there's no need
for a hubbub.
Tell those corgis
to be quiet please.
Her Highness feels
quite at ease
with an eightlegged
ambassador
making a grope
towards her royal soap.
Indeed, the Queen
is truly amused.

And wasn't it a spider
who introduced
a lesson of some moral use
to Scotland's old King Bruce?
Yes, spiders have been known
to be mentors to a throne.
They have a sense of honour
in their common stealth –
a message she will ponder
before the Commonwealth.

So sitting the spider
snugly beside her
the Queen enquires
of the spinning one:
why heavy lies the hand
that holds the sceptre
and lightly moves the finger
that twirls the spindle?

But all she gets for answer
is a twinkling parable

of thread

Nansi Airobics

Spin and weave
bend those knees

spiral torso
low as limbo

tangle limbs
in webs of vertigo

the dance ends
when your thread runs out

Anancy's Thoughts on Couples

Teeth and tongue must bite
when they share one mouth-roof.

Two buttocks must brush
when they share the same bed.

New cloth comes from the rub
of spindle and thread.

Apply the law of the loom
to warp and weft of bedroom.

Aunty and Uncle Nancy's Pillow Talk

1

Lovergirl, I have trade winds in my back
And weave myself down to where nature cracks.
I blow down to where your roots most ready
Till all your islands empty their contents

Loverboy, when I wine my continent
And move the coastline of my waist
I mek you break away like Trinidad
Till all your peaks weak with my conchshell taste

2

Lovergirl, the match wide open, sun hot
and the field is set with deep gully.
I spinning down your legside spot
But I holding back my googly.

Loverboy, I'm in hipship testmatch shape
And ready for spin or swing attack.
My wicket turf is paradise patch
So bowl your length and line. Find the crack.

3

Talking slack
is sweet foreplay,
says Aunty Nancy
And keeps sleep tight
says Uncle Nancy

Is so dem spiderlimbed lovers
boastify in the wee
hours of the night

dreaming of geography
and cricket lovely cricket

and the world looks better
from a spinning delta.

How Aunty Nansi Singularly Widened the Debate on Plural Identity

What a high-brow-knitting controversy
when Aunty Nansi on topical TV show
presented herself as proof of plurality.

Dressed in a side-splitting sari
a red gold and green necklace for Selassie
and snazzy tartan shawl for the cold

Aunty Nansi sat up to her full height
face straight to camera in front row
her stockings laddering the limelight

And with fingers nail-polished lilywhite
same as she'd womanicured her every toe
she gesticulated to gentleman host:

'Now Mr Kilroy, you tell me
Am I Afro-Celto-Euro-Indo
or just beautiful byproduct of cosmos?'

And with her question spiralling like a ghost
Aunty Nansi took the opportunity
to wave hello to her folks across the galaxy.

Inter-City Anancy

Never one for trainspotting and birdwatching

on the London-Edinburgh inter-city
(it may have been the 20.00 hours
I can't remember exactly)
I stumbled on a less stressful hobby

spotting old English ladies knitting
watching their white fingers deftly spitting
image of spider's dancing serendipity

and between the silence of needles
and the clipping of tickets
I heard once more the call of the mythic

and for a split second, it was eyes lulled
by epiphany in a ball of wool

My hairy knuckles felt an atavistic twitch
for knitting to a spider would be a cinch.
I thought of joining their crochet class

but closed my eyes and let the landscape pass
basking in the thought of timeless bridges
built with the frailest stitch.

Anancy's Website

e-mailed
she-mailed
on line
on website

the globe
is caught
in a net
of linear
light

while over
their heads
the dark
sub-text
of my web

goes unread

Anancy's Voice Mail

Hello, you're through
to the voice mail
of Anancy.
Lucky you.
I'm here
and not here
if you get my drift.
My head
in one continent
my foot
in another
my waist
mid-Atlantic.
But leave your message
loud and clear
in any language
and I will mail
my voice forthwith.
Thank you for
calling in-transit.

How Aunty Nansi Reshuffled Prospero's Books

Aunty Nancy show
up bright and early
at the house of Prospero.
Hear how she perky up her voice:

I'd gladly make cocoa
for you dearest Prospero
but you mixing me
up with another lady
named Miss Wendy Cope.
No, I do my travelling by rope
and I come to help reshuffle
them books in your library –
restore the voices they muffle,
in a manner of speaking.
That's why to keep abreast
of the literary canon
I read all the works by Anon.
And I always stack my reading
tome by tome hexagonally
straight from floor to ceiling.
Let's start with M for Mythology.
I find alphabetical disorder
a little more appealing.

Soon Aunty Nansi
busy talking to sheself in Twi
told Prospero in her sweetest lisp:
I done twi-dy up the library.

Then in a crisp
crackling voice, ailing Prospero said:
How about some heavenly reggae
round the baseless fabric of my bed?

And with her wisp
of waist and throwback head
Aunty Nansi replied: I like it
when you talk rude
but may I remind you
that the tea not even brewed.

So it was Prospero's turn
to put the kettle on
and pour a pot for two.
They talked of weather, inflation,
immigration, poll tax,
but never got around
to the matter of Sycorax
for that roots-woman was taboo
and familiarity
breeds familiars
like black cats and spiders
embodied out of thin air...

Aunty Nansi, are you still here?
Have my eyes gone all deceiving?
Or is that you reading from the ceiling?

And so their raves and revels ended
one by sleep was grounded
one by thread ascended.

Anancygrams

The sky they say is the limit.
But the ceiling's a good start.

*

Whenever I weave my bridge
that's my home.

*

Lil river make big sea.
Small axe cut down tall tree.
Short step start long journey.
Thin pen write fat history.

*

Talk some, write some,
keep some in the archives
of the heart.

*

The Haitian proverb says:
When the anthropologist arrives
the gods depart.

*

It ain't over till the fat lady sings.
It only begins when the thin spider spins.

*

Swing low sweet chariot of thread.
Travel begins inside the head.

*

When seven threads of colour begin to glow
All shall look towards Spider's rainbow.

*

Some say white is white, some say black is black.
Spider finds hope in a tiny grey crack.

*

World is wide
as web spun.

Spider work
never done.

After a playful bout
of stargazing
and galaxypondering
I Nansi come to the conclusion
that the milky way
is a web of constellation
and since as above so below
it logically follows
that earth and people
are a web of connection
so what some call coincidence
I call webpath crossing
or to put it another way

Web: one small syllable uttered
bears the weight
of the universe

Trembling thread of fate

LIMBO DANCER IN DARK GLASSES

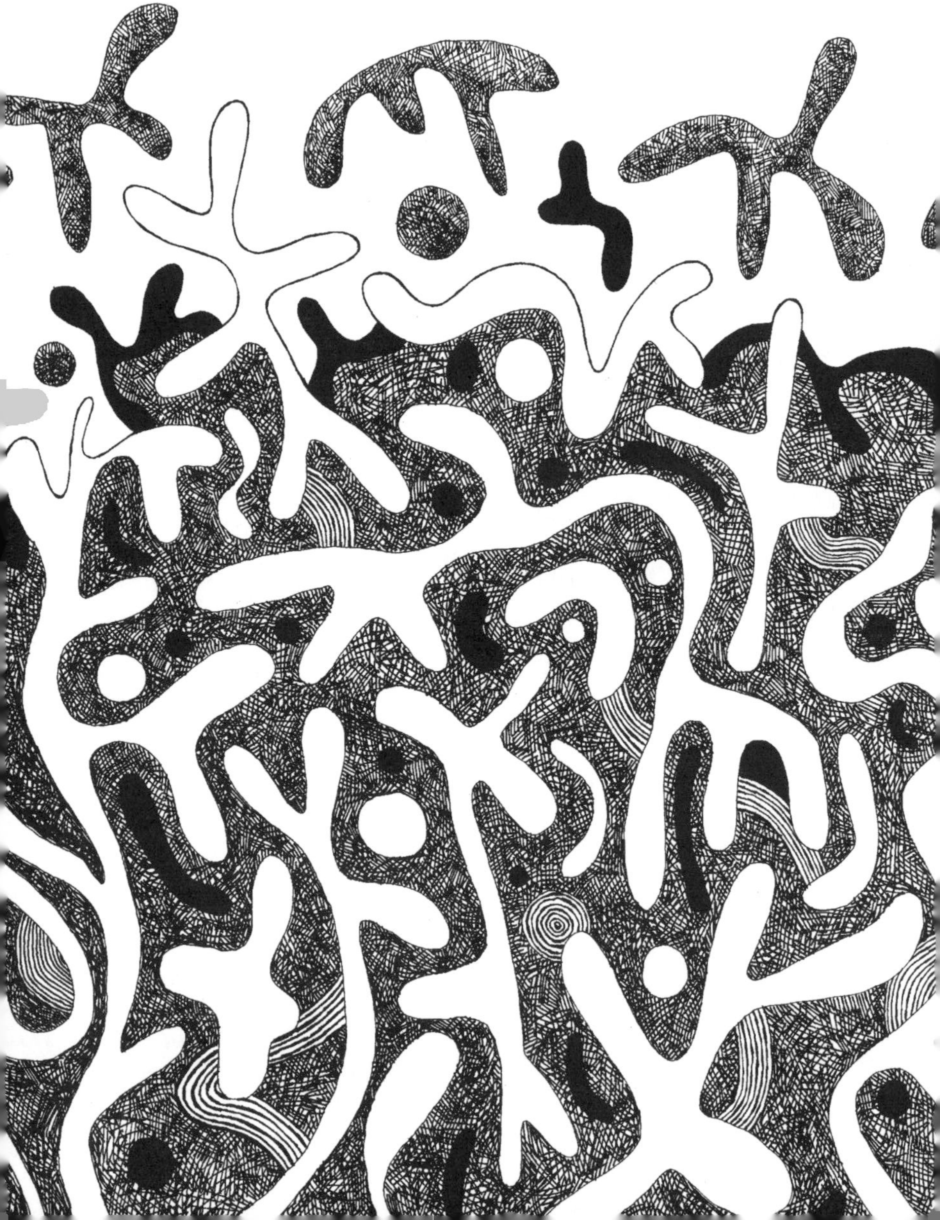

Whether male or female
who can be sure

who can pin a gender
on this limbo dancer

who can dare decipher
this human spider

dismembered under
a deck of fire

Limbo Dancer's Wombsong

From timeless waters
of the primal womb
I was dancing soon

believe me it was fun
in the primal womb
like great balloon

though my limbs were tender
I'd bend backwards over
giving a mighty quiver

sometimes I'd stretch umbilical cord
like an extra limb
& revel dancing under

such sweet contractions
my mother said she felt
she wanted to carry me forever

Name

Mother of universe
drunk with thirst
for movement

arched her belly like a bow
stretched every limb to limitless
saying when time ripe
for giving birth

let this child of mine be called limbo

Limbo Dancer's Morning

I

In the morning when I wake
I give good stretch
& my limbs know no limit

my fingers stroke sands of Africa

my toes curl around lianas
of Brazilian rainforest

& in movement I find rest

this is no idle boast
no guarded secret

merely survival

II

Then again some mornings when I wake
I seem to lose all sense of space
& in so doing become space

my limbs merge with wind
sound floods my every fibre

my toes grope for holes of flute
my fingers pluck skin of drum
my lips breathe into strings
of armadillo

& universe whispers   limbo

The Reason

Because they know
I have centuries of bending behind me

because they know
I can bend so low
barbed wire cannot hold me

they felt a concentration camp
would not be safe enough for me
& though 6 million Jews did not agree

they decided to send me to Chile
& there they held me facedown in a stadium

I thought they would have smashed my knees
as they did Victor's hands
instead they simply called me missing

But because they know
I have centuries of bending behind me

they felt a stadium
would not hold me for very long

so they transferred me to Southern Africa
where I was placed in solitary confinement
but it was the same in that other continent

I thought they would have manacled my ankles
as they had done with Biko

But because they know
centuries ago
I had learnt to live with manacles

they decided to banish me
to a living hell
& the name of Mandela rang a bell

But because they were told
they had got the wrong man/or the wrong woman

since to them my sex was indecipherable
& in any case unimportant

& knowing I was capable of a million disguises

they gave the order to shoot on sight
without question
anything seen bending backwards

so if you should see anywhere
a rifle aimed towards the rainbow

you must know
I limbo dancer

am the reason

Question Mark

Whether I move in light
or dark
the powers that be
have a question mark
over me

they're no longer sure
whether to interpret
bending over backwards
a position
of supplication/or aggression

Once

Once they gave a smile
& called me ethnic

once they looked amazed
& called me kinetic

once they applauded
& called me magic

now they say get out from under there
we know you're hiding under that stick
come out now or we'll shoot you hear

Limbo Dancer & the Press

The Western press never took kindly
to limbo dancer gyrations

described by one paper as deadly
to international relations
hazard to territorial integrity

With head perched in highlands of Guyana
knees spread wide in Venezuela

neck arched somewhere in Argentina
toes touching Falklands

hands cleaving chill Afghanistan air
legs bent bowlike across USSR

limbs doing frenzied to & fro
between Southern Africa & Lesotho

& when limbo dancer cried in Namibia
a limbo of tears descended in Soweto

Cynics called this a cheap acrobatic stunt
the western press cried Soviet propaganda

From the Kremlin there was no comment at first
but things really got worse
when limbo dancer rippled under
Berlin Wall to applause of tourists

To the Soviets this was no acrobatic stunt
this was bourgeois & decadent

No one thought of calling limbo dancer
simply a child of the universe

Limbo Dancer at Immigration

It was always the same
at every border/at every frontier/
at every port/at every airport/
                                        of every metropolis

The same hassle
from authorities

the same battle
with bureaucrats

a bunch of official cats
ready to scratch

looking limbo dancer up & down
scrutinising passport with a frown

COUNTRY OF ORIGIN: SLAVESHIP

Never heard of that one
the authorities sniggered

Suppose you got here on a banana boat
the authorities sniggered

More likely a spaceship
the authorities sniggered

Slaveship/spaceship/Pan Am/British Airways/Air France
It's all the same
smiled limbo dancer

Now don't give us any of your lip
the authorities sniggered

ANY IDENTIFYING MARKS?

And when limbo dancer showed them sparks
of vision in eyes that held rivers
                                it meant nothing to them

And when limbo dancer held up hands
that told a tale of nails
                                it meant nothing to them

And when limbo dancer offered a neck
that bore the brunt of countless lynchings
                                it meant nothing to them

And when limbo dancer revealed ankles
bruised with the memory of chains
                                it meant nothing to them

So limbo dancer bent over backwards
                                & danced
                                & danced
                                & danced

until from every limb
flowed a trail of red

& what the authorities thought
was a trail of blood

was only spilt duty-free wine

so limbo dancer smiled
saying I have nothing to declare
& to the sound of drum disappeared

Beware of Limbo Dancer

On the walls
of toilets
in your cities
you scarred graffiti

NO USE STANDING ON THE TOILET SEAT
THE CRABLOUSE HERE IS CAPABLE
OF A POLEVAULTING FEAT

& in the same breath
you scribbled

BEWARE OF LIMBO DANCER

& you warned your sons
never marry limbo dancer

& you warned your daughters
never marry limbo dancer

but it was to no avail
it was casting water on duck back

your sons & daughters
set off on the track/on the trail/on the tail
of limbo dancer

but not taking any chances
you burnt sticks of incense
sprinkled garlic on the floor
even super-concentrated fairy liquid
resorted to every act of cheap commercial magic

but it was to no avail
it was casting water on duck back

I limbo
dancer
is the omen
like spilt wine
your eyes beheld
but did not read
the sign

Look again this time inwards
& understanding shall be yours

I limbo
dancer
is the dream
your ego
does not know
lies buried
in your spine

Seek & it shall rise

Why?

I

In your plastic frenzy
you spend time & money
on sessions of therapy
to discover that education
begins in the womb

Why didn't you come to me?
I limbo dancer
could have told you so for free

II

According to one branch
of your psychology
the source of all energy
springs from the LIBIDO

Please let them know
that's not the way
to spell LIMBO

Limbo Dancer at the Orgy

What are you staring at?
Why are you making passes?

Tell me have you never seen
a limbo dancer in dark glasses?

Not My Style

Name spelt out in neon lights
name blaring out from mikes
posters to send the town wild

no that's not my style
I limbo dancer
keep a low profile

Out of the Question

Once in my life I did make a blunder
when one psychiatrist looked at me with wonder
& said I don't care if your name is limbo dancer
that couch is not meant for dancing under

Besides you dance like one inviting copulation
& that for me is quite out of the question

Take a Tip

Here's news for all you lovers

not to bruise each other
with games of ego

but to fuse each other
with flames of limbo

to lose self in sweet surrender

take a tip from one
who like water
has danced under
many bridges of time

Getting High

Some get their kicks
from gin & tonics

some get hooked
on harder stuff

for me it's enough
to wash myself
in colours of the spectrum
& at signal from drum

bend towards the cosmic needle

Not Again

Some called it histrionics
some called it Third World tactics
but after what happened
at the last Olympics

a decision was taken
to debar
limbo dancer
from the Commonwealth Games

we can't have anyone setting flames
to the highjump bar

Limbo Dancer's Reading Habits

Limbo dancer reads the *Wretched of the Earth*
bending over backwards

Limbo dancer reads *How Europe Underdeveloped Africa*
bending over backwards

Limbo dancer reads Che Guevara's diary
bending over backwards

Limbo dancer reads Angela Davis' autobiography
bending over backwards

Limbo dancer reads *Capitalism & Slavery*
bending over backwards
& has chained every word to memory

But limbo dancer also reads the *Kama Sutra*
bending over backwards
as well as *The Joys of Natural Childbirth*

Some believe this is what makes limbo dancer
capable of sustaining multiple revolutions

Limbo Dancer at the Conference Table

Mr CHAIRman, Mr CHAIRman
haven't you forgotten your TABLE manners?

The fork is not for the soup
or pinching ladies/legs
underneath the table

Accusing eyes seek me out
as if to say BEWARE OF LIMBO DANCER
but am I not seated on the table
arms folded at peace between my knees?

And Mr Chairman please
how much longer must we wait
how many more hours
for matters arising out of minutes?

Can't you see the dispossessed
are beginning to fidget?

I thought the purpose of this meeting
was to discuss the fate
of the needy & the hungry
how much longer must we wait?

And why have you asked me to sit on top the table
when all you needed was a paperweight?

O no Mr Chairman
I am not your specimen/token/problem

I shall not be ripped off/
taken for a ride/screwed to the dust/
given a six for a nine/
manhandled/blacklisted/blackballed/blackmailed

I do not mix my words or my drinks
I believe in calling a spade a spade

And Mr Chairman
even as I hear myself speak
before the sentences fall from my very tongue
like dead ash on ground

I see of words used without question
you have fashioned a trap
as you did for the buffalo
not so long ago

But Mr Chairman
I who have moved an ocean
with knees of limbo
now move this motion

& will bend your language
to a new echo

Limbo Dancer's Soundpoem

Go
down
low
low
low

show
dem
what
you know
how
know

let
limb
flow
flow
flow

as sound
of drum
grow
grow
grow

& body
bend
like bow
bow
bow
limb/bow
low
low
low
limb/bow

Limbo Dancer's Mantra

LIMB/BOW

Pronounce dem
two syllable
real slow
you hear me
real slow

LIMB/BOW

Savour dem
two syllable
till glow
spread from head
to tip of toe

LIMB/BOW

Contemplate dem
two syllable
in vertigo
of drum tempo

LIMBO

Meditate on dem
two syllable
calm as zero
vibrate to sound
let mind go

& forget the stick
I tell you
don't think about the stick

that will take care of itself

Rainbow

When you see
de rainbow
you know
God know
wha he doing –
one big smile
across the sky –
I tell you
God got style
the man got style

When you see
raincloud pass
and de rainbow
make a show
I tell you
is God doing
limbo
the man doing
limbo

But sometimes
you know
when I see
de rainbow
so full of glow
& curving
like she bearing child
I does want know
if God
ain't a woman

If that is so
the woman got style
man she got style

Limbo Dancer's Memo

Chained in limbo
watch a body flow
from web of darkness
into light

historical memory
linking/me back
          to human cargo
          a seed of light
          in limbo

Again I say to you
you don't need to own
radio/or video
to know that they lay low
our prophets of hope
who dare voice
the suffering
          of the ghetto

I promise not to use words
like oppression/exploitation
genocide/nuclear waste
ecological suicide/
for you have heard them
so many dog-eat-dog times

But upon the wicked ones
I cast curse
as did my mother before me
mother of universe

                    limb of my limb/mover of galaxy
                    limb of my limb/bow of harmony

I queen of limbo
I king of limbo
world without end
will not bend

to fixed roles
of their status quo

I limbo dancer
too supple
for their double standards

to be/or not to be
passive/aggressive/
feminine cry/masculine cry not/
play with dolls/play with guns/
follow emotion/follow logic/

all so rigid/all so slick
but jill be nimble
jill be quick
jill dance under the limbo stick

I queen of limbo
I king of limbo
I whose knees
have spanned the Atlantic

will grant the blind ones
their commercial breaks
their sugarcoated con/trick

But rulers of the world
before you dance with me
you must first overthrow your ego

Rulers of the world
O hear me/take heed
for you know/& I know/& the people know

limousines do not bleed

Look

Do not look for limbo dancer
in nightclubs of Port of Spain/or Montego Bay
for there you'll find only limbo dancer's shadow

look among the masses
joining endless queues for bread
for limbo dancer/has known the urgency/of hunger

look for that body bent like a bow
among the vigil for the New Cross dead

for limbo dancer/knows too well/the joys of parenthood
trapped/screaming fire/a living hell

look for those limbs linked like song
to 30,000 voices of women at Greenham Common

for limbo dancer cherishes the bloom of sisterhood/
& remembers well the pain of rape/a slaveship womb
like unwanted missile

look for the arching neck
among the children of Soweto
& the miners of Gdansk

for limbo dancer has known the rupture of brotherhood
herded together/eyes washed in blood

wherever sisterhood & brotherhood join in struggle
there you will find a rainbow of protest

Sign

I

At another time
at another place
had I walked on water
or changed a stick to bread
they would have called me saviour
yet hanged me on cross of wood

At another time
at another place
had I come
leaping on a stick
they would have called me witch
& burnt me at stake

Now many oceans later
I have a different fate
Now they pay dear
to see me leap under
a stick of fire
& call me entertainer

It isn't so much
that times have changed
it's just that mistakes
are now more profitable.

II

Limbo dancer
will not take no
for an answer

Limbo dancer
will posture
under your pillow

bending backwards under
your very dreams

III

You might well have said come inside
& arched yourself in welcome

you might well have opened your skin
to the probing drum

you might well have greeted the sensation
of bending over backwards

for even if you are unwilling to do so now
limbo dancer will return as sure as blood
in fact will never leave your footsteps

one day prepare to cross centuries
in a matter of inches

At the Crossroads

1

Limbo dancer
will not take no
for an answer

Limbo dancer
will posture
under your pillow

bending backwards under
your very dreams

2

You might well have said come inside
and arched yourself in welcome

you might well have opened your skin
to the probing drum

you might well have greeted the sensation
of bending over backwards

for even if you are unwilling to do so now
limbo dancer will return as sure as blood
in fact will never leave your footsteps

one day prepare to cross centuries
in a matter of inches

3

Meet me at the crossroads
and I limbo dancer
will tell you my story.

That is if you can bend
low enough to hear me.

MAN TO PAN

Pan Recipe

First rape a people
simmer for centuries

bring memories to boil
foil voice of drum

add pinch of pain
to rain of rage

stifle drum again
then mix strains of blood

over slow fire
watch fever grow

till energy burst
with rhythm thirst

cut bamboo and cure
whip well like hell

stir sound from dustbin
pound handful biscuit tin

cover down in shanty town
and leave mixture alone

when ready will explode

The official church, as part of its drive to eliminate "foreign" religions, outlawed the drums. But no celebration in Trinidad works right without rhythm. 'Bamboo tamboo' stick bands were devised to fill the musical gap. The bands were hundreds of young people, each carrying a bamboo pole, nine to eleven inches thick and four to six feet long. A deep hollow sound, varying with the size of the bamboo, was made by pounding the open end of the stick on the ground.

JANE SARNOFF
(notes to LP *The Sound of the Sun*)

On new ground we scatter old drum seeds
letting them shape a destiny of sound
unburdening the iron in our blood.
Thunder roots new voice in steel
and lightning seams metal with song.

Who would have dreamed that Shango heart
would beat this far would follow us
across strange water to stranger earth
rising to thunder from oildrum rust?

I

Messages pour
from the throat
of the drum

Welcome
the stranger at the door
Beware
the enemy's scorpion stealth
Embrace
the birthsong of the newborn
O brave
the threshing hand of death
Gather
the swollen joys of harvest

From hill to forest
the voice of the drum speaks
and no one taught the leaves
to listen
but echoes cling to their green ears
like dewdrops

and the river whispers
atum/pan
atum/pan

II

once upon an umbilical time
no one need
be told to heed
your windblown warnings
your newborn blessings

once long long ago
in the shadow
of the Golden Stool
we could read
the fingers roll
on stretched skin

once in the bowel
of another land
long severed long gone
we understood
the vowels
of the drum

once the heart of wind
bore a scroll
of sound
and the drummer's palms
unfolded syllables
like magic pods

III

O gather gather
as hands moved by spirit
blessed by fire
spurred by goathide phantom
lingering shadow of the drum

now stir
the slumbering tongue
within skins of steel

O feel man
de riddum
        atum/pan atum/pan
        is steel/pan
            feel man
            feel man

Those drums!
Those drums!
Demonic sounds
of subversion.

Obviously
their conversion
to Christian ways
was merely skin deep.

In their heathen sleep
and wildly mumbled praise
to savage gods...
Ogun Shango
whatever their name...

It's all the same
mumbo-jumbo

O no no
definitely
the drum
will have to go.

They mean to license we tongue,
yes, that's why they ban we drum.
They don't have to find reason
to throw people in prison

But if they think we go stay dumb
since they decide to ban we drum
then they got to think again
cause we go rage like burning cane

CANBOULAY CANBOULAY
we celebrating today.
Stickfight in full swing
WHO'S ME FRIEND DON'T JOIN DE RING

How they go stop people giving vent
to a whole mass of frustration?
De stricter de government
de smarter de population

Well, too bad, they don't have a clue
they forget nature give we bamboo
growing wild and growing free,
bamboo band belong to you and me.
Is part of we ancestry, ah telling you

So we go cut bamboo at full moon
to beat out we sorta tune
then strike up bottle and spoon.

Tamboo-bamboo is here to stay,
no, they can't take that away

If they think we go stay dumb
since they decide to ban we drum
then they got to think again
cause we go rage like burning cane

TAM/TAM   TAM/TAM
BAM/BAM   BAM/BAM
BOO/BOO   BOO/BOO
TAM/BAM   TAM/BAM
BAM/BOO   BAM/BOO
TAM/BOO   BAM/BOO
TAMBOOBAMBOOTAMBOOBAMBOO

riddum growing green
for fullmoon sweetness
ripen in we hand
tamboobamboo band
carry we back to another land

Now we making a fresh start
cause Shango navel string
bury in we heart
so people let me hear you sing

for sugarcane we bleed
but bamboo reed
satisfy we need
to make drum talk

TUNE/BOOM   TUNE/BOOM
BADOOM/BADOOM/DOOM/DOOM
LOOM OF SOUND

we go pick it
from bamboo clump
and thump it
on de ground

FULLER
CUTTER
we go pick it
we go lick it
we go scratch it
SCRATCH/SCRATCH
CLAX/CLAX
CLACKATY/CLAX

TO HELL WITH DE GOVERNMENT AXE

we go trick riddum
out of god mouth
with bamboo drum
we ladder of sound

so hear me god/hear me good
prepare the sky
                    to greet the mud

Who is me?
look ole man
all come fuh
mih woman.
Who is me?
I is she master
I is master
of Iron an
it in mih blood

ABDUL MALIK
Pan Run

DELIVER
hammer
blow
on steel/
DELIVER
steel
belly
groan/
DELIVER
steel
skin
stretch/
DELIVER
steel
flesh
shudder/
DELIVER
steel
womb
pulse
& burn/
DELIVER
till
birth
cry
of steel
mudder
say
PAN
bornNN
PraisSSEE GoddDD

Born naked
clothed only
in fountain of fire

baptismal oil
on your black brow

we name you
PAN
bury your navel string
in metal web of sound

O what sweet toil
what joy
to watch you now

spread your wings

Let each hammer blow
shaping
concave womb
of old oildrum
be the voice
of Shango
thunder

Let each lick of fire
tempering
blue-hot metal
be the splintered tongue
of Shango
lightning

Let this sweet kiss of fever
Let this blackness of mirror
Let this websong of spider

to panman's
shaman
touch surrender
surrender

is the sinking   for the taste of fire
of metal
is the cleaving   to the thrust of chisel
of a feeling
is the weaving   in a web of sound
of a dream
is the sounding   in old oildrum
of a scream
is the drumming   to a beat of steel
of a heart
is the grounding   to tones of blood
of a hurt
is the pounding   to tunes of love
of a rage
is the wounding   by slash of stars
of a night
is the grooving   by trickles of light
of blackness
is the moving   to the embrace
of a man
of
PAN

Rivulets of melody
spread out
like lines of destiny
spread out
from me palm
of flesh
to you palm
of steel

Man to pan
ah feel
we grow as one
from root to sky
ah feel
we flow as one
when blood meet iron
in one suncry

Rubber tip
twin
sticks
lip/
PING
metal
drip/
PING
sweetness
keep/
PING
riddum
sweep/
PING
sound
from steel
flip/
PING
round
de ring
like humming
bird
wing
Man
you know
de ting

PING
PONG

For hands honed by pan grooves
hammerblows on metal are actsoflove
but listen well for tones of rage and hurt

Watch that miracle of sound flow
from hands attuned to mystery of steel.
Bloodriddum tells him what is real

In oildrum darkness
watch them hands chisel notes like stars well/seamed
temper rustgloom to pan turner's dream

Yes, hammerblows on metal are actsoflove
but listen well for tones of rage and hurt

Pan
you is one
wo/
man
I won't
mess
with
one lil
caress
and you
obsess
mih
but I don't
mind
so long
they oppress
mih
wha wrong
if you
possess
mih?

Look
possess
mih
and free
mih

Steelpan
dark web
of Anancy

black pool
of ancient
memory

help break
this chain
of history

help beat out
this pain
in yuh sweet womb

mek me
born again

Spiderwheel of steel
n
i n
p i
s n
g
d
t n
h u
r o
e s
a
d f
s o
through middlepassage memory
holding continents
in hub of melody
spin spiderwheel
h
t c
i u
w n
n
n i
i n
p g
s
of anancy
threads
of stunning
sweetness

When you hear
dem silksmooth notes
spiralling
from steelweb
and feel
dem raindrop threads
of sound
weaving riddum to blood
you know
is not for nothing
they call it
spiderpan

When I tell you
spider got wing
you think is lie.
Well wait till
you see pan fly.

They say oil don't spoil
is not me say so
is de politician.
I wonder if they know
oildrum don't spoil either.
It mek home for spider.

Watch inside that pan
somebody tell me
if ah seeing right.
Is a spider
weaving melody
or the rays of the sun
coming out at night?

Spider you ain't tired?
If you ain't watching me
from the ceiling
you busy weaving
harmonies under me.
Now when I touch me heart
ah feeling spider web.

Flight of fingers
flight of wingtip rubber
through a landscape of grooves
through a limbo of steel

Fly panman fly
you know this skyline web
of hummingbirdsound
like the palm of yuh hand

Fly?
It ain always so easy
to fly above slum/mess
even with wings of tenderness

It ain always so easy
to break out this damn prison
of history
even with instruments of reason

wrench this slave/shadow/chain
clinging like bad/blood
in the basin of mih memory

The weight of centuries heavy.
Man, I up to mih neck in scars

But black night mek for stars
and stars born to shine

So when you see me caressing steel
you must know I hold the dream of pan
to ease the itch/and switch/of knifeblade

MAGISTRATE: All this pan-beating
is a downright nuisance.
Where can it all be leading
but to decadence?

PANMAN: Your Honour, you talking high sounding
but if you could feel the pounding
of the righteous rage
running through mih veins
you would know why I beat pan.

MAGISTRATE: Righteous rage? You? Just sixteen?
A youngster still green
with his mother's features.

PANMAN: If Africa is mih mudder
then mih heart is a map of wrinkles.
Your Honour it would make you shudder
to know I feel old as centuries.

MAGISTRATE: What has all this got to do
with the big hullabaloo
of beating pans all over the place?
Making yourself a public disgrace.

PANMAN: Is the burden of mih race.
When I beat pan
I beat out the fury
of a history
I make but didn't write.

MAGISTRATE: That gives you no right
to go breaking the law.
All this pan-beating
is much too coarse too loud too raw.

PANMAN: Them that living high
have their ears up in a cloud.
They look down on roots sound
and what they fraid they brand too loud

but when yuh bread well-butter
especially with the knife of power.
Man, you could sentence
half a nation to the gutter.

MAGISTRATE: Since the gutter is where they belong
don't expect them to discriminate
between right and wrong.
The law must keept them in their place.

PANMAN: Is the burden of mih race.

MAGISTRATE: More the burden of indecency
if you ask me. Hooligans
miss the meaning of the word rowdy,
they understand knives and guns
and of course disturbing people with pans.

PANMAN: I won't lie
I won't deny
that panman
and policeman
don't clash

For that matter
blade does flash
between panman
and panman

But hear this.
Take away pan
and too much blood
go flow in this land

And I go tell you why.
When I stare
at the web/eye
of pan
and pan stare back at me
man, I outstare history.

I rise above
the sea of poverty

At least for a time
ah touching love
ah healing hurt
ah forgetting survive
ah feeling paradise
ahhh…

MAGISTRATE: Paradise like hell!
Look, take him away
I had enough for one day.

Goatskin tongue
could set fire
to streets

so ban de drum
mek it dumb
Congoman must
know he place

see dem spider/web/groove
in oildrum mirror?

hear dem sweetsweet notes
flowing pingpong river?

is steel/pan
feel/man
de riddum

is Anancy
curl up in sound
is sky
come to ground
is dustbin
taking wing
is bamboo roots
on fire tamboo/bamboo
womb
of new/world/sound

is pan/ping
is pan/pon
is pan/gong
is pan/boom

pipe organ
in oildrum belly

how rubbertip nipple
could suckle sound so
Beethoven to kaiso
shantytown sound turn concerto

is another classic
Anancy trick

Carnival is all that is claimed for it. It is exultation of the mass will, its hedonism so sacred that to withdraw from it, to be a contemplative outside of its frenzy is heresy.

DEREK WALCOTT

Carnival is inconceivable without music. The appropriation of the masquerade by blacks following emancipation produced a long search for a type of musical instrument suited to the festival, to the culture of the people, and to their resources, both material and financial. That search was conducted in a social climate of hostility and repression. It was a search that continued for one hundred years and ended in glorious fulfilment with the invention of the steel band.

ERROL HILL

Street turn river
flowing riddum
street turn fire
sparking sweat
street turn volcano
erupting colour

JeeessSSUS pan in prime
wine if you wineEEING
grine if you grineEEING
move yuh body in time

the only crime
the only sin

is standing still

But cynic as I am

With foot fixed to earth
I watch them re-enact this mass-birth

Rooted to lack of motion
from the shores of a safer gaze
I do not enter their tramping ocean

If crime it is
to contemplate outside the frenzy
then call my stillness heresy

But O what temptation sweet
impels me to the pull of pan
shifting earth from under my feet

De road goin groan today
We ain't care we ain't care
Every man woman child must have their way

Street going blaze with tramping feet
We ain't care we ain't care
Brain gone wild when music so sweet
We ain't care we ain't care
So long as de band don't stop play
De road going groan today

Steelband riddum swing we head
We play in mas till we drop down dead
Is mas in you ass or clear de way
Now ain't time to gaze and dream
Now is time to let off steam
So if you come to contemplate
Then shove down going be your fate

So you better don't wait
Come and join de band
Wine yuh waist shake yuh hand
Cause when band coming down is stampede
And when band clash man go bleed
Bottle knife cutlash go flash
When bacchanal start better make a dash
If not prepare to meet stick with stick
Lash foh lash lick foh lick

I suppose it's necessary
this release of energy
this yearly tyranny of the blood
this tramping flood
of feet gone mad
(or if you prefer 'bacchanal bad')

I suppose one might even say
it's therapy
but I stand the risk
of heresy
I suppose it's more like
theatre of the will to war
(or is this going too far?)

What else should I say
when reality leaves me no choice?
Perhaps I should just raise my voice
and like the exploding mass
say pan hour come at last
all power to pan
all power to the people

But what would matter to them?

O fuck it man
just join de band

Earth moving to greet feet
sun smiling down from sky
yellow spider from blue ceiling
as if it know the feeling
that today is de day
we going trick history
in steelbeatfrenzy
in this rivermotion of colour
today is de day
pan going seize power

In a rain of sounds
rebounding
from belly to brain
in a rain of sounds
unbound
by shanty/town
or history/wounds
steelpan
steelpain
steelrage
steelsweetness
unchain
a rain of sounds
and watch
rusting memories
drown

Hear it at Hosein
worship of Tadjah
Hear it at Shango
lord of thunder
Hear it in the crashing/cymbal/roar
                    of dragon dance
Hear it in the waterfalling
                    earthprayer
                    of Cariban/Arawakan
                    scattering
                    nomad/seed/blessings
                    far back
                    as Behring crossings

echo
of heartbeat
THE DRUM

shadow
of thunder
THE DRUM

hunger
of volcano
THE DRUM

goatskin stretched
bridging continents

in a circle of sound
woven of skin/of blood/of gong

in this circle of sound
centuries meet
foot touching ground
after wilderness of water

in this pan/mirror
bloods mingle in steel
energies reflect

twistings/of/history

sticks once rubbed for fire
now beaten for melody

linking urges
older than memory

and the pain purges
in the act of beating
as limbs surge
to the call of steel/skin

Reflections
of black
moons
tuned
to filaments
of sound
fragment/disperse/entwine
in a web
of harmonies
reflections
of drumbeat
chainsweat
knifeedge
memories
reflections
in dark
poolface
of pan
disturbing
the gaze
of centuries

Is more than a snapshot mirror
reflecting panman face
in a mood of concentration
complete with perspiration

Is more than a straw/hat/native
making a merry steel show
whilst he catching ass to live
in some bad/john/ghetto

Is more than knocking out a tune
on a sunbeach/package/tour
with rum flowing like blood
and the body calling for more

No/
pan deeper than that man
                    is a heap of history in you hand

Ogun
Ogun
you think is fun
beating iron
in the sun?
carrying iron
in we blood
like how de man
carry he cross
of wood?
you think is fun
you think is fun

but riddum
is the devil
pounding
the anvil
of mih brain
drumming
out the pain

so we moving on
we moving on
till clank of dawn
we moving on
we moving on
with sound of iron
for we companion
we moving on
we moving on

till earth scream
birth/scream
with de dream
of iron
for we crown

Dat was de sweetest music Trinidad ever hear,
An' high in de air, leading de band
Was de sweetest Tenor dis side of heaven,
It was Sugar beating he heart out,
Bend over he pan like a statue of stone,
He eh hearing, he eh seeing, he eh feeling,
De world for he was de sweet tenor in he hand
An' he beat, an' he beat, an' he beat

PAUL KEENS-DOUGLAS
Sugar George

When I crouch over
with mih head inside a pan
no use talking to me man
cause I ain't hearing/
Mih ear too full-up
with the sound of lightning
tearing
darkness into splin/
ters/
Is Shango fingers
playing havoc with mih brain
No use talking to me man
when I crouch over
with mih head inside a pan
The whispers
I hearing
is the softer side of thunder
Know wha ah mean?
And if you wonder
where ah been
well I making a rounds
of the heavens
watching God full-eye
through circle rims of light
that could pass for metal
in the dark
if you not seeing right/
Now I turnin down
a side street
of a night
name history
and if you can't see me
just follow the panbeat
and you won't go wrong
but don't blame me pardner
if you get loss
cause mystery is pan father
like spider web self/

No use calling out mih name
I can't hear you man
not when I crouch over
with mih head inside a pan/
Now ah following
spider footstep
across the water
dodging
like Midnight Robber
with steelsound
for mih dagger
and the only gun
ah carrying
is O/gun
dream of iron
on new ground/
So you could brandish
yuh whip
how much you wish
if you think you go see me slip
you got to think again
cause Shango thunder
binding whipcrack
to a stammer
and history
is a bitch
I go lavish
with flowers of steel
till she memory
mesmerise with sound
and she wish
she ship
did run a/ground
But too late
too late is the cry
and these rims
of darkness
leaking light
from mih eye
is more than rings
of pain
or lack of sleep/

Is a long deep
moving
to a/wakening
a hurtful growth
And I got to hold the birth
of vision
springing
from this web
of steel
singing
from the depth
of night
till ah feel
earth
move with love
groove with light
and after centuries
of turning
mih back to the sun
burning like whip
in mih memory
ah learning
to embrace
another sun
with rays
of melody
under me/
So no use talking to me man
when I crouch over
with mih head inside a pan
cause I ain't hearing/
Mih head inside the sun
and the water
searing
the rim
of mih eye
is no ordinary sweat/
Is Shango sweating fire
to a kiss of steel

God hear me is you I talkin to
God you know you smart foh so
Man you is master of mamaguy
All this time I thinking you up there somewhere
sit down on yuh throne with yuh long white hair
watching down from the sky with yuh wisdom eye
I thinking you is a fella born to live high
keeping company with planet and rainbow
too high to take on lowdown life in ghetto
But I never see thing so
I ain't know all this skytalk is just skylark
to keep me in the dark
God you know you smart bad
So long history had you on the run
only now I know you is the one Ogun
hiding all this time in old oildrum
and living right here in Trinidad
When I want to pray they tell me lift up yuh head man
but all this time yuh throne right here inside a pan

When you talking pan
you talking power
ah telling you pardner
you get mih language?
or you still crossing
de middle passage?

Mind how you holding that pan
is a mirror in you hand
drop it and so help me god
is 400 years crosses...
you say you ain't superstitious
well drop it if you name man

how you mean pan sweet
ain't is humming bird
heartbeat?

They say the sound of pan
sinful
like the human race
so get ready the fire
and baptism oil/
but ah warning you Fadder
pan is one baby
you better baptise good
anoint she belly
till she brow pure as blood

I ain't know head or tail
bout chromatic scale
and to me octave
is a word dat rhyme with slave/
but dat is what they tell me
they tell me tenor pan
extending two octave
upwards from middle C/
well dat is news to me
ah got to take dey word for it/
but when ah hit
out a melody from memory
they say he earsound good
riddum in he blood
he musical sense keen
it must be in he genes/
ah think ah know wha dey mean/
but ah does smile to de tenor pan
and de tenor pan give me one wicked smile
as if to say tell them me octave
extending upwards
to give thunder praise
and one day you must ask them for me
if lightning begin from middle C

Lick pan
with trick
of hand

is old old
magic
in new land

stick
that know
the taste
of fire
when hunger
foh heat
brace man
is no
stranger
to the ways
of iron

so
lick pan
with trick
of hand

Ogun
don't take
long
to wake

Beat it out man
beat out the hurt
beat it out
to riddum of steel/
feel
panblood flow
watch the dream
grow
from things unshaped
to real/
beat it out man
beat it out
beat out the rape
of the whip
shadow
the burn and blow
on gaping skin/
beat it out man
beat it out
beat out the weight
of history
scar/and/hate
beat it out man
beat it out
beat out the bleed
And spill
of seed
to waste/
beat it out man
beat it out
beat out
a new message
from de middle/
passage
womb of riddle/
beat it out man
beat it out
beat out the burden
of history
sound

beat it/heal it/shape it
confound
wounds
with vision

In 1956 Spree Simon visited Ghana and passed on his skill in pan making. With him the ancient drums of Shango having crossed the Atlantic, returned to Africa in a new guise after a sojourn of two centuries in a strange land

ERIC PAYNE
The Steel Band Story

after so many turns
after so many failures
touch him

he smiles

hold him
he rages

murder him
he shatters you

your thunder has come home

KAMAU BRATHWAITE
Shango

was like a return to me
was spree finding spree
not in chains but free

was all o that and deeper
was the dream
returning to the sleeper
was the stream
returning to the river
was the river
returning to the sea
was all o that and deeper

it kinda hard to explain
after 400 years of pain
but to tell you de truth
i ain't think ah go looking for
any sorta roots
i from trinidad
and ah like it bad
i ain't know wha ah go looking for
or wha to expect
i ain't go to resurrect
any ghosts i long time forget
it ain't as if i go hoping for
a welcome home fête
like dry mud hugging oletalk rain
de mudderland opening she hand:
'eh eh where you been all dis time boy?
i hear you playing steelband
since you cross de atlantic
you is one big man
you forget is i teach you to beat stick
anyhow i forgive you
i know wha four century
could do to you memory'

no it wasn't like that
it kinda hard to explain
after 400 years of pain
but even though ah say spree boy just go
do like limbo

let you body flow
don't put fancy notion in you brain
yet ah find when ah step off de plane
it kinda hard to explain

was like a return to me
was spree finding spree
not in chains but free

was all o that and deeper
was the dream
returning to the sleeper
was the stream
returning to the river
was the river
returning to the sea
was all o that and deeper

ah say yes well ah tell you pardner
dis is it you reach dis is africa
you go lick down palm wine like rum
you go hear plenty drum
you go hug up earthriddum woman
then ah tell meself
you start again?
wipe dem fancy notion from you brain
don't bring you bad
habits from Trinidad
till to africa
take it cool take it cool
born slow born slow
400 years you been in de womb
by now you should know
to born slow
born slow

forget fancy notion
limbo in slow motion
and as ah turn to touch ground
with this offering of steel sound
ah feel a funny feeling
as if ah dreaming
as if ah been here before
it never happen to you?
as if ah go walk down a street
and bound to meet
up with somebody ah know
manette jules fisheye
one o dem fellas go stop and say
'eh eh spree you here too?
like trinidad move out?
wha going on nuh wha going on?
leh we fire one leh we fire one'
ah had was to tell meself
spree keep you head on
you is a long long way from john-john

still lah get de feeling again
it kinda hard to explain

was like a return to me
was spree finding spree
not in chains but free

but even as ah tread de peace
of mudder ground
ah couldn't help wonder if it go be hard
to find mih way around
ah mean it ain't like walking through panyard
was more like walking through the middle
of another passage
with four century excess luggage
but sudden so in the middle
i remember the answer to the riddle
ONE RED ONE BLACK
ONE LICKING THE OTHER BOTTOM
POT ON FIRE
POT ON FIRE

you wrong
you wrong
answer spider
try again
try again
ONE RED ONE BLACK
ONE LICKING THE OTHER BOTTOM
then in the groove of mih brain
the answer come
P-A-N P-A-N
PAN/ON/FIRE
PAN/ON/FIRE
you hear me spider?
but spider didn't reply
and ah swear to god
in de circle of me eye
ah see spider leave he web
and taking flight to the sky
ah say jesus wha is dis?
you eye playing tricks
ah say spree boy you mus be weary
is jet lag from the journey
you better get some sleep
like a axe splitting mih brain
it kinda hard to explain
but wha ah thought was spider thread
was shango climbing
on a chain
of sound
with a smile
of lightning
and mih foot root to mudder ground
ah didn't have to go no further
ah didn't have to wait for thunder
ah know
was a return to me
ja ja romy-o
was spree finding spree
ja ja romy-o
not in chains but free
ja ja romy-o
and as ah stand up deh

in that web of light
ah feel like panorama night
and ah hear meself say
oyo oyo
oyo shango
ah glad to see you man
accept this offering
of pan
is you drum come home
wha i borrow
i return
oyo oyo
oyo shango
accept this offering
of pan